THE HOUND OF THE BASKERVILLES

SIR ARTHUR CONAN DOYLE

LEVEL

RETOLD BY NICK BULLARD
ILLUSTRATED BY ALEX OXTON
SERIES EDITOR: SORREL PITTS

⚠ Contains adult content, which could include: sexual behaviour or exploitation, misuse of alcohol, smoking, illegal drugs, violence and dangerous behaviour.

PENGUIN BOOKS

UK | USA | Canada | Ireland | Australia
India | New Zealand | South Africa

Penguin Books is part of the Penguin Random House group of companies whose addresses can be found at global.penguinrandomhouse.com.
www.penguin.co.uk www.puffin.co.uk www.ladybird.co.uk

Penguin Readers (Level 3) edition of *The Hound of the Baskervilles* published by Penguin Books Ltd, 2026
001

Original text written by Sir Arthur Conan Doyle
Text for Penguin Readers edition adapted by Nick Bullard
Text for Penguin Readers edition copyright © Penguin Books Ltd, 2026
Illustrated by Alex Oxton
Illustrations copyright © Penguin Books Ltd, 2019
Cover illustration by Despotica. Front cover design by Coralie Bickford-Smith
Cover image copyright © Penguin Books, 2007

Penguin Random House values and supports copyright. Copyright fuels creativity, encourages diverse voices, promotes freedom of expression and supports a vibrant culture. Thank you for purchasing an authorized edition of this book and for respecting intellectual property laws by not reproducing, scanning or distributing any part of it by any means without permission. You are supporting authors and enabling Penguin Random House to continue to publish books for everyone. No part of this book may be used or reproduced in any manner for the purpose of training artificial intelligence technologies or systems. In accordance with Article 4(3) of the DSM Directive 2019/790, Penguin Random House expressly reserves this work from the text and data mining exception.

Printed and bound in Great Britain by Clays Ltd, Elcograf S.p.A.

The authorized representative in the EEA is Penguin Random House Ireland, Morrison Chambers, 32 Nassau Street, Dublin D02 YH68

A CIP catalogue record for this book is available from the British Library

ISBN: 978–0–241–78650–5

All correspondence to:
Penguin Books
Penguin Random House Children's
One Embassy Gardens, 8 Viaduct Gardens, London SW11 7BW

Penguin Random House is committed to a sustainable future for our business, our readers and our planet. This book is made from Forest Stewardship Council® certified paper.

Contents

People in the story	4
New words	5
Note about the story	6
Before-reading questions	6
Chapter One – Mr Sherlock Holmes	7
Chapter Two – The Baskerville family	13
Chapter Three – A journey to Devon	19
Chapter Four – The Stapletons	25
Chapter Five – Letters to Sherlock Holmes	30
Chapter Six – More questions	38
Chapter Seven – Death on the moor	44
Chapter Eight – The picture	52
Chapter Nine – On the moor	60
Chapter Ten – Home in London	67
During-reading questions	70
After-reading questions	72
Exercises	73
Project work	77
Glossary	78

People in the story

Sherlock Holmes

Doctor Watson

Doctor Mortimer

Sir Henry Baskerville

Mr Stapleton

Beryl Stapleton

Mr and Mrs Barrymore

Laura Lyons

New words

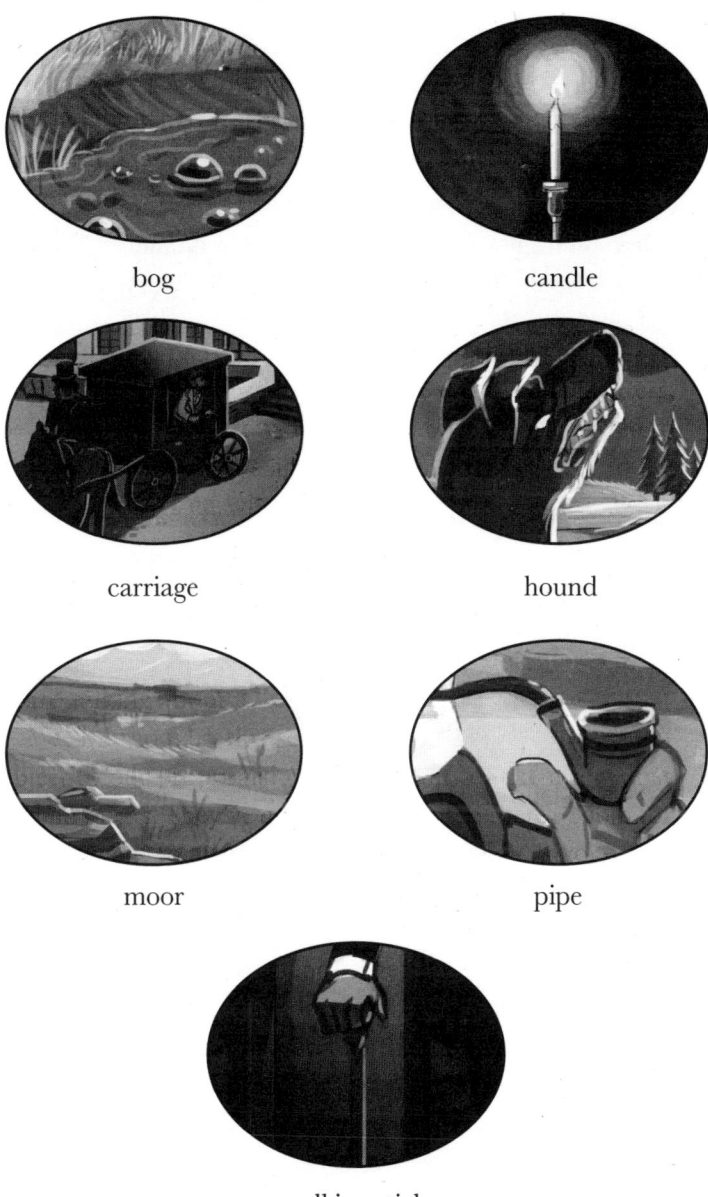

bog

candle

carriage

hound

moor

pipe

walking stick

Note about the story

Sir* Arthur Conan Doyle was born in Edinburgh, Scotland in 1859. He was a doctor and he wrote stories about Sherlock Holmes. Holmes is an intelligent **detective**. His friend, Dr Watson, helps Holmes with his **cases** and writes about them. Usually, people with problems come to Holmes in his flat at 221B Baker Street in London.

The Hound of the Baskervilles tells the story of the Baskerville family. The family have a big house on Dartmoor, a large moor in the south-west of England. The moor is an empty, wild place and few people live there. It has hills, rocks and **dangerous** bogs. In the middle of the moor is the famous Dartmoor **Prison**. **Prisoners** sometimes **escape** from the prison.

The Baskervilles are an old, important and rich family. The oldest man in a family like this has the word *Sir* before his name – so we have Sir Hugo, Sir Charles and Sir Henry in this story. *Sir* is also the word **servants** use to speak to the people that they work for.

Before-reading questions

1 Look at the cover and the pictures inside the book. What animal is important in the story? What do you know about it?

2 Choose three people from the "People in the story" on page 4. How old are they, do you think, and what do they look like?

*Definitions of words in **bold** can be found in the glossary on pages 78–80.

CHAPTER ONE
Mr Sherlock Holmes

My friend, Sherlock Holmes, does not often get up early because he works late into the night. But I **visited** him this morning, and he was sitting at the breakfast table.

"We had a visitor yesterday, Watson," said Holmes, passing me a walking stick. "I didn't see him because I was out, but he left this stick. What docs it tell you?"

I looked at the stick **carefully**. "Well, Holmes," I said. "His name is here. It's Mortimer, and he's a doctor. He's not a young man so he needs a stick. The stick was cxpcnsivc, but he's used it for many years. I think that he lives in the country – town doctors usually have newer, cleaner sticks."

"Very good, Watson," said Holmes, taking the stick from me. "But he's *not* an old man – he doesn't need this stick. He has a dog, and the dog often carries it. Look at the middle of the stick – the dog's teeth held it there. But there's someone at the door. Dr Mortimer has come back."

A tall young man with glasses came into the

room with a small dog. His eyes moved to the stick.

"Are you Dr Mortimer?" asked Holmes, passing him the stick.

"Yes. Thank you, Mr Holmes," the doctor said. "It's my favourite stick, and I don't want to lose it. It was a present from some very good friends."

"Now, Dr Mortimer," said Holmes. "You didn't just come here for your stick. This is my friend, Dr Watson. How can we help you?"

"I live in Devon, Mr Holmes," answered Dr Mortimer. "My home is near Baskerville Hall, on Dartmoor, and I was a friend of **Sir** Charles Baskerville. He lived in Baskerville Hall, but he died three months ago. Before he died, he told me the strange story of the Hound of the Baskervilles."

"The Hound of the Baskervilles?" said Holmes. "How interesting. Please tell the story to us."

"In the year 1742, Sir Hugo Baskerville lived in Baskerville Hall. He was a terrible man. He **fell in love** with a young woman, but she didn't love him. One night, Sir Hugo saw the young woman, and **chased** her into the moor. Some of his friends saw him. They chased him, but he **disappeared** into the night. After a few minutes they **heard** a terrible cry, and they found the young woman on the wet ground – she was dead with **fright**. And near her lay Sir Hugo. An enormous black animal was standing over him. It looked like a huge hound, but it was bigger than any hound on this Earth. The animal was attacking Sir Hugo with its teeth, and soon he was dead, too. The animal ran off. Its mouth was red with Sir Hugo's **blood**."

Dr Mortimer looked at Holmes. "What do you think?" he asked.

"This may be interesting," said the **detective**, "but only to lovers of old stories."

"I can tell you more," said Dr Mortimer. "For more than a hundred years, people have talked about a strange hound on the moors. It chases and attacks men from the Baskerville family. Two years ago, Sir Charles Baskerville came to live at Baskerville Hall. Sir Hugo's brother was his grandfather's grandfather. I was Sir Charles's friend and his doctor, and I often visited him because he had a **weak heart**. In the months before he died, he became a very worried man. He knew the story of Sir Hugo, and he was sure that he was in **danger**, too. He heard loud noises on the moor at night – the **howls** of a huge hound. Other people heard these howls, too, and they sometimes saw a huge black hound running across the moor. One night, Sir Charles and I were standing outside the Hall. We both saw a large black animal in the hills."

"I see," said Holmes. "Can you tell me more about Baskerville Hall and Sir Charles?"

"Baskerville Hall is on the moor," said Mortimer, "and there aren't many **neighbours**. Sir Charles wasn't married, and he lived with two **servants**, Mr and Mrs Barrymore. On the evening of his death, he went out for a walk in his garden, but he didn't come back. Mr Barrymore was worried, and he went outside – and found Sir Charles near a **gate** between the garden and the moor. Mr Barrymore called me, and I came to Baskerville Hall. Sir Charles was dead. There was no blood on him, and I thought that he died because of his heart problems. His pipe was on the ground near the gate, and between Sir Charles and the gate, I saw footprints."

"Of a man or a woman?" asked Holmes.

Dr Mortimer looked at us strangely, then his voice went very quiet. "They were the footprints of an enormous hound!" he replied.

CHAPTER TWO
The Baskerville family

Holmes looked at Dr Mortimer carefully. "Are you sure about the footprints?" he asked.

"Yes," answered Dr Mortimer. "They were enormous. Farmers use sheepdogs on the moor, but these footprints were much bigger than a sheepdog's feet."

"And were they near the body?"

"Yes."

"And the pipe was next to the gate?" said Holmes.

"Yes. I think that Sir Charles stood by the gate for five minutes to smoke his pipe."

"I have another question," said Holmes. "Who will **inherit** Baskerville Hall?"

"Sir Henry Baskerville, Sir Charles's nephew, will inherit the Hall," answered Mortimer. "Sir Charles was the oldest of three brothers. The second brother died young, but he had a son, Henry. There was a third brother, the youngest, Rodger. He was a wild young man like Sir Hugo, and he didn't want to stay in England. He wanted to make money, so he went to Central America, but he died there.

"Henry left England, too, and went to live in Canada, but he's coming back because he inherits everything. He took a ship across the Atlantic, and he arrives in London today. I'm meeting him in an hour. But is he in danger from this hound, Mr Holmes? Is Baskerville Hall a **dangerous** place for him?"

"I need to think about that," said Holmes. "Go and meet Sir Henry and take him to a hotel. Come here with him tomorrow morning at ten o'clock. But say nothing to him yet about the hound."

"Thank you," said Mortimer, and he stood up. "We'll see you tomorrow."

"One more question," said Holmes. "Some people saw the hound in the days before Sir Charles's death. But did anybody see it after that?"

"I've heard nothing."

"Thank you, Dr Mortimer. We'll meet again tomorrow."

I left Holmes for the afternoon and came back in the evening. The air in his room was thick with smoke, and there were papers everywhere.

"Watson," said my friend. "I haven't left my room all day, but I've drunk a lot of coffee, smoked and thought a lot. Look at this." He pointed at a large **map**. "Baskerville Hall is here, in the middle of the map, and there aren't many houses near it. There's the small village of Grimpen – Dr Mortimer lives there – and two farms. There's a famous **prison** at Princetown, but it's twenty kilometres across the moor. Now let's think about the death of Sir Charles. He had heart problems, we know that, and he was afraid of the moor because of the hound. So why did he stand near the gate to the moor for five minutes?

Was he waiting for something or someone? Tomorrow we'll have some questions for Sir Henry."

―――――

Dr Mortimer and Sir Henry Baskerville arrived at ten o'clock the next morning. Sir Henry was a man of about thirty, with dark eyes and a light brown beard.

"This is Sir Henry Baskerville," said Dr Mortimer.

"It's good to meet you, Mr Holmes," said Sir Henry. "Some strange things have happened in the last few hours, and I want to talk about them." He put a letter down on the table in front of us. I read the address: *SIR HENRY BASKERVILLE, NORTHUMBERLAND HOTEL.* It looked like a child's writing, but I guessed that it was an adult's work.

"Who knew that you were at the Northumberland Hotel?" asked Holmes.

"Only Dr Mortimer," said Sir Henry.

"Someone is following you," said Holmes. He opened the letter, and we all read it: *Do not go on the moor. It is dangerous for you.*

"Someone cut these words from a **newspaper**," said Holmes, "and used them to make this sentence.

Look at the letters. They come from *The Times*, I think. The person made the sentence quickly, because the words aren't straight on the paper. Was this person worried or frightened? Now, is there anything more, Sir Henry?"

"Yes. I've lost a brown boot. I put my boots outside the door of my room last night because I wanted someone from the hotel to clean them. But this morning there was only one boot. They were new boots, too. I bought them yesterday. But why did you want to see me, Mr Holmes? It wasn't for my boots. You want to talk about something more important than that."

"Dr Mortimer," said Holmes. "Can you tell us your story from yesterday again?"

Dr Mortimer told the story of Sir Hugo, Sir Charles and the enormous hound, and Sir Henry listened carefully.

"Now, Sir Henry," said Holmes. "What do you think? Do you still want to go to Baskerville Hall?"

"Why would I not want to go?" asked Sir Henry.

"There seems to be danger," replied Holmes. "But we need to learn if it is from this hound or from a person."

"I heard about the hound many years ago,

and I never thought that it was a danger," said Sir Henry. "I thought that nothing could stop me from going to live in my family home. It's very important to me. But my uncle's death changes things. I need time to think, and I'd like to talk to you again before I go. Will you and Dr Watson have lunch with me at my hotel at two o'clock?"

"Yes, of course," said Holmes. "We'll meet later."

The two men left, and Holmes jumped out of his chair. "Quick, Watson, let's follow them!"

We ran out of the flat and into Baker Street. Mortimer and Sir Henry were about two hundred metres in front of us. They stopped to look in a shop window. Holmes and I stopped, too, and so did a man with a big black beard on the other side of the street.

"You see, Watson," said Holmes. "That man with the beard is following them, too. Let's look at him more closely."

But the man turned and saw us, and he ran into a smaller street. There were a lot of people there, and he disappeared.

"But we know that we need to find a man with a big black beard," I said.

"But was it a real beard, Watson?" asked Holmes.

CHAPTER THREE
A journey to Devon

Holmes and I walked to the Northumberland Hotel for lunch with Sir Henry Baskerville. He was waiting for us, and he showed us an old black boot.

"They've stolen another boot!" he shouted angrily. "First, they took a new brown boot, now they've taken an old black one. But I'm sorry, Mr Holmes, this isn't important."

"It may be important, Sir Henry," said Holmes. "It explains something. I don't understand it yet, but each little thing helps to give us a bigger picture. But do you still plan to go to Baskerville Hall?"

"Yes, I'm going on Saturday."

"That's a good idea. We know that someone is following you in London, and I can't watch everyone in an enormous city. You may be safer at Baskerville Hall because there aren't many neighbours. Dr Mortimer, did you know that a man was following you and Sir Henry yesterday?"

"No."

"This man has a black beard. Are there any neighbours on Dartmoor with a black beard?"

"Barrymore, the servant at Baskerville Hall, has a black beard," Dr Mortimer replied. "But he's in Devon now, I'm sure. His father and grandfather worked at the Hall, too. They're a good family and we can **trust** him."

"Did Barrymore get any money when Sir Charles died?" asked Holmes.

"Yes," said Mortimer. "He and his wife got five hundred pounds each."

"Interesting," said Holmes.

"But Sir Charles left money to other people, too. He left me a thousand pounds," said Mortimer. "I hope that I'm not a **suspect**!"

"And how much money goes to Sir Henry?" asked Holmes.

"Nearly a million pounds," answered Mortimer.

"I see," said Holmes. "Sir Charles was very rich. And – I'm sorry to ask this question but it's very important. If Sir Henry dies who will inherit this money?"

"Rodger Baskerville, Sir Charles's youngest brother, is dead. He never married, and he had no children," said Mortimer. "There's a third cousin in the north of England. Not many people know about him. But because Sir Rodger had no children, this third cousin will inherit everything. But I met him once and I know that he doesn't want Baskerville Hall or any money."

"Sir Henry," said Holmes. "You should go to Devon on Saturday, but you mustn't go **alone**. I'd like to go with you, but I've got important work in London. Watson, can you go with Sir Henry?"

This was a surprise, but I'm always ready for an adventure. I was also happy that Holmes trusted me. "Of course," I answered.

On Saturday morning, Holmes came to the train station with me. "I want you to visit all the neighbours of Baskerville Hall," he said. "I trust Dr Mortimer, and I think that we can trust the old cousin in the north of England. One of the neighbours is our suspect. Visit them all and write to me about them."

"What about the Barrymores? Do we send them away from the Hall?" I asked.

"No. They're suspects, of course, but there are other suspects. Do you have your gun?"

"Yes."

"You may need it. Keep it with you all the time."

Dr Mortimer and Sir Henry were waiting for us at the station.

"Do you have any news?" asked Holmes.

"No one has followed us," said Mortimer. "We've watched everyone carefully."

"One thing," said Sir Henry. "I've found my new brown boot."

"Have you found the old black one?" asked Holmes.

"No."

"Interesting," said Holmes. "Well, goodbye, and have a good journey. And don't forget to write to me, Watson."

The train travelled to Devon, and Sir Henry, Dr Mortimer and I talked and watched the hills and fields out of the window. After three or four hours we were crossing Dartmoor. We got out at a small station, and I was surprised to see policemen there.

"Why are the police here?" I asked.

"A man has **escaped** from the prison at Princetown," said Mortimer. "He's Selden, the murderer – a very dangerous man. He's on the moor and people are very frightened."

A JOURNEY TO DEVON

We drove in a carriage across the wild, empty moor. In the evening light, I saw nothing but hills, rocks and a few small trees. The police stopped us on the road, and they looked at us carefully. After half an hour, Dr Mortimer pointed out of the window.

"That house is Baskerville Hall," he told me.

I saw a large old house. It was alone on the moor, with no houses near.

Dr Mortimer went home to his wife, and Sir Henry and I went into Baskerville Hall. Mr and Mrs Barrymore came to the front door to meet us. Mr Barrymore was a tall man with a large beard. Mrs Barrymore was a small, friendly woman.

"Welcome to Baskerville Hall, Sir Henry!" said Mr Barrymore. "Would you like dinner now?"

"Yes, please," answered Sir Henry.

Inside, the Hall was a dark, unhappy place. The rooms were high, and there were pictures of Sir Hugo and the other Baskervilles on the wall. Everything felt old and sad. We talked a little at dinner, but I was happy to go to bed. Before I went to sleep, I looked out of the window at the moor. There were rocks and a few trees, but no houses. Under the cold moon it was a sad, empty place.

I did not sleep well. The house was very quiet, but in the middle of the night I heard a strange noise. It sounded like a woman, and she was crying. I was sure that the noise came from inside the house. Then the crying stopped. I listened for half an hour, but I did not hear it again.

CHAPTER FOUR
The Stapletons

The next morning was sunny and beautiful. Sir Henry and I had breakfast by the window and looked out across the moor. I nearly forgot that last night the place was sad and dark.

"We were tired and cold, yesterday evening," said Sir Henry, "but today we can feel happier."

"You're right," I said. "But I heard something strange in the night. It sounded like a woman. She was crying."

"I heard something in the middle of the night, too," said Sir Henry. Barrymore was in the next room, and he called to him. "Barrymore, did you hear a woman crying last night?"

"No, Sir Henry," Barrymore replied, entering the room. "There's only one woman in the house – my wife. She wasn't crying."

But Barrymore was **lying**. I saw Mrs Barrymore after breakfast, and her eyes were red and tired. Why was she crying at night? And why did her husband lie to us? I remembered the man with the beard in the street in London. Was that man

Barrymore? But what **motive** did Barrymore have to kill Sir Charles? I couldn't think of one.

After breakfast, I walked into the village of Grimpen. It was a fine walk by the side of the moor. Near the village, I heard someone running up behind me, and a voice calling my name. I turned to see a young man with light hair and a moustache.

"Excuse me, Dr Watson," he said. "I'm a friend of Dr Mortimer and he's talked about you. My name's Stapleton. Is Sir Henry at the Hall this morning?"

"Yes, he is," I said.

"Do you and Sir Henry know the old story of the hound on the moor?" asked Stapleton.

"Yes, we've heard it."

"I don't **believe** that stupid story," said Stapleton. "But Sir Charles believed it. It worried him a lot, and I think that he died of fright because he saw a dog that night. His heart was weak, and he was frightened of dogs. But what do you think?"

"I don't know yet."

"And what does Sherlock Holmes say about it?" asked Stapleton.

"I can't answer that."

"Is Mr Holmes coming to Devon?"

"He has work in London," I told him.

"If you have any suspects in the **case**, you can ask me about them," said Stapleton.

"Thank you," I said. "But I'm not a detective. I'm just here to visit Sir Henry."

"I understand," said Stapleton. "But we're only a short walk from our house. There's a **path** here across the moor to it. Would you like to come and meet my sister?"

I started to say no, because Holmes wanted me to stay by Sir Henry's side. But Holmes also wanted me to study the neighbours, so I followed Stapleton on a small path.

"I know the moor well," he told me. "I'm interested in **butterflies** and there are a lot here. The plants are often dark and brown, but look at that." He pointed to a green place on the moor. "It's the Great Grimpen Bog, and it's very dangerous. Wild horses and other animals run into it, and they can't get out. I know safe paths into the bog, and I find butterflies there. But listen, there's a horse there now. It's dying in the bog."

I heard the loud **scream** of a horse. We walked

towards the sound and saw it. It was going down into the bog and there was nothing we could do for it. But then I heard another noise. A strange howl was coming from the moor and it sounded even worse than the horse. It was the strangest sound I've heard in my life.

"What's that?" I asked.

"People hear that and talk about the Hound of the Baskervilles," said Stapleton. "But I think that it sounds more like a bird than a hound."

We arrived at Stapleton's house, and his sister, Beryl, was there to meet us. She was a beautiful woman, but with her dark hair and face, she didn't look like her brother. Stapleton showed me the house. It was small, but comfortable, with many books and pictures.

We sat down to a cup of tea. "We came here last year," Stapleton told me. "We had a school in the north of England, but it closed, so we moved here. I love this moor."

We all went outside, and I said goodbye to Stapleton and his sister. But after I left, something strange happened. Beryl Stapleton ran after me and stopped me.

"Dr Watson," she said. "Please tell Sir Henry to

go back to London. Now."

"Why?"

"It's dangerous for him here. But don't say anything to my brother about this."

CHAPTER FIVE
Letters to Sherlock Holmes

Holmes asked me to write to him from Devon. Here are two of my letters.

Baskerville Hall, 13th October
My dear Holmes,

*As you already know from my last letter, there's an **escaped** prisoner on the moor. He's a dangerous man, and people are frightened. I'm a little worried for the Stapletons because they live alone on the moor.*

Sir Henry has visited the Stapletons often, and I think that he's falling in love with Beryl Stapleton. She's a beautiful and intelligent woman. But Mr Stapleton doesn't seem to want Sir Henry and Beryl to be alone together. I don't understand him. Sir Henry is a rich man, but he's also very kind, and he will make an excellent husband for a woman like Beryl.

On Thursday, Dr Mortimer and the Stapletons came to lunch with us. After we finished eating, we went into the garden of Baskerville Hall.

"Where did my uncle die?" asked Sir Henry.

There's a small white gate, and a path into the moor. Mortimer pointed to the gate. "It was here," he told us.

I tried to picture Sir Charles that evening, standing with his pipe. Is it possible that something, or someone, came off the moor and frightened the old man?

I'm worried about the Barrymores. They're suspects, but I can't find a motive. But why was Mrs Barrymore crying the first night I was in Baskerville Hall, and why does she often have red eyes? I decided to watch the Barrymores carefully.

Last night, I woke up at about two o'clock in the morning because I heard someone walk past my bedroom door. I opened it quietly and looked out. Barrymore was walking into one of the empty bedrooms with a candle in his hand. I followed him and watched. He was looking through a window into the night. Then he held the candle up to the window and looked again. He waited a long time. I went quietly back to my bed, and after a few minutes, I heard him leave the room.
Your friend
Watson

Baskerville Hall, 15th October

My dear Holmes,

Quite a lot has happened in the last two days.

First, I took Sir Henry to the empty bedroom and showed him the window.

"You can see the moor very well from here," I told him. "Barrymore was looking across the moor at something."

"I've heard him in the night, too," said Sir Henry. "We'll follow him next time. But now, I'm going out for a walk."

*"I'll come with you," I said. "Holmes doesn't want you **alone** on the moor."*

"I'm sorry, Watson," said Sir Henry. "But I must walk alone. I'm visiting someone special."

I decided to follow him.

*Sir Henry left the hall, and he walked on a path into the moor. I waited a little, and went after him. After a few minutes I saw him on the path, and he was walking with Beryl Stapleton. I **hid** behind a large rock on the hill above them and watched. They stopped and talked quietly, but I couldn't hear them. Suddenly, Stapleton was there, running on the moor path. He stopped and shouted angrily at Sir Henry. Then he took his sister's arm and walked with her across the moor.*

Sir Henry stood sadly with his head down. I ran down the hill to him.

"Watson," he said, looking surprised. "Why are you here? Did you follow me?"

"I'm sorry," I said, "but I had to come after you. It may be dangerous on the moor."

For a second he looked angry, but then he smiled. "Did you see her brother?" he asked. "He was very angry with us."

"Why?" I asked.

"I don't know. Am I crazy, Watson? I don't understand. I just want to talk to Beryl. I can be a good husband to her."

"No, you're not crazy, Sir Henry. She's an intelligent and beautiful woman."

"But Stapleton doesn't want me to touch her. Why? I asked her to marry me, but he arrived, and she didn't have time to answer. Then he took her home."

"It's all very strange," I said.

But that afternoon, Stapleton came to see us.

*"I'm very sorry, Sir Henry," he said. "I was wrong this morning. I love my sister very much, and I don't want to lose her. But I know that's not right. I was surprised and angry to see her with you. I think I need a little time to understand things. But can I **invite** you and Watson to dinner with us on Friday?"*

We understand Stapleton a little better, now, and I have also discovered the Barrymores' secret. Last night, Sir Henry and I waited in my bedroom. At three o'clock in the morning, we heard steps outside the door. We followed Barrymore to the same empty bedroom. Barrymore was at the window with his candle. His face was against the glass, and he was looking out over the moor. Sir Henry walked up to him.

"What are you doing, Barrymore?" he asked.

"Nothing, sir." But he was very surprised. "I was holding a candle to the window."

"But why?" asked Sir Henry.

"Don't ask me that, sir. It's not my secret."

I had an idea, and I took the candle from Barrymore. "He's sending a message," I said. "Let's see if there's an answer."

I held the candle to the window and looked across the moor. Suddenly, we saw another light out in the night.

"There's the answer," I said.

"Move the light across the window," said Sir Henry.

I moved the candle, and the light on the moor moved, too.

"There's someone there," said Sir Henry. "Who is it, Barrymore? Why are you sending messages?"

"I can tell you, sir," said a voice behind us. It was Mrs Barrymore.

"My brother is on the moor," she told us. "We take food and old clothes to him. Our candle tells him that we have food to bring. He answers with that light."

"Then your brother is—"

"Selden, the prisoner. He's a murderer, I know that, but he's also my little brother, and I love him. He escaped from prison, and he's hiding on the moor. I must help him. He wants to go to the sea, find a ship and escape to another country."

"Is this true, Barrymore?" asked Sir Henry.

"Yes, sir, every word."

"Well, Barrymore, family is important, but you're helping a murderer. We'll talk about this in the morning. Go back to your room."

The Barrymores left, and Sir Henry and I went to the window. We looked across the moor at the light.

"Where is he, do you think?" he asked me.

"I think the light is on Black Hill."

"That's only a mile or two. And he's waiting there for his food. He's a dangerous man, Watson, and he may attack people. I'm going to catch him."

"I'll come with you," I said.

"Then get your gun and put on your boots."

In five minutes, we were on the path. It started to rain, and then we heard a strange noise come across the moor. It was the howl that I heard before, with Stapleton, by the Great Grimpen Bog.

"What's that, Watson?" asked Sir Henry.

"I don't know. But I've heard it before."

"Is it a hound?"

"Stapleton thinks that it's a bird," I told him. "But I think that it's a hound."

"It's a terrible howl," said Sir Henry.

"Shall we go back to the Hall?" I asked.

"No. We've come for the murderer!"

We walked through the dark night. We could see the light and it was getting brighter.

"But where's Selden?" Sir Henry asked, quietly.

Then we saw him, in the rocks. He saw us, stood up quickly and threw a large stone at us. It hit the rock above my head. Then he ran away across the moor. He moved quickly and disappeared into the dark night. There was no time to use my gun.

Sir Henry and I started to walk home, but we saw something very strange across the moor. It was a tall, thin man. He was not the murderer because Selden was short. I called to Sir Henry, and pointed at the man, but he disappeared.

"Maybe he's a policeman," said Sir Henry. "There are a lot of them on the moor. We'll talk to the police tomorrow. Selden may stay near here, because he needs food from his sister."

That is my news for now, Holmes. I hope to have more in my next letter. But I hope, too, that you can soon come to Devon and help us.
Your friend
Watson

CHAPTER SIX
More questions

The next morning, I finished my letter to Holmes, and then Sir Henry and I talked to Barrymore.

"I'm sorry that you chased my wife's brother last night," said Barrymore. "Please don't tell the police. He's going to South America."

"But he's a dangerous man," said Sir Henry. "There are people living on the moor near here."

"He won't attack anyone, sir," said Barrymore. "If he attacks someone, the police will know that he's here. He'll do nothing until he finds a ship. It will kill my wife if he goes back to prison."

"What do you think, Watson?" Sir Henry asked.

"Let him go," I said. "If he's out of the country, then it's better for everyone."

Sir Henry turned to Barrymore. "All right, Barrymore. We won't go to the police. But Selden must leave England soon."

"Thank you, sir," said Barrymore. "Now there's something I must tell you about Sir Charles's death. I haven't told anyone this before. I **suspect** that he went to the gate that night to meet a woman."

"Which woman?" I asked.

"I don't know her name, but she wrote him a letter. I found it in his room. She only finished it with *L. L.* – but it was a woman's writing."

"What did it say?" asked Sir Henry.

"It said, *Please be at the gate at ten o'clock tonight. L.L.*"

"Do you have the letter?" I asked.

"No, sir, I didn't know that it was important."

"Thank you, Barrymore," said Sir Henry.

After Barrymore left, Sir Henry turned to me. "What do you think?"

"We were in the dark before, but now it's darker," I said. "We need to find L. L."

I wrote to Holmes. The next day was cold and wet, but that evening I went out on the moor. I thought about poor Selden, out there in this terrible weather. And then I thought about that other, taller, man. Where was he now?

As I walked back, I met Dr Mortimer. He was driving home, and I got into his carriage.

"Dr Mortimer, you know most of the people near here," I said. "Do you know a woman with the letters L.L. in her name?"

He thought for a few minutes. "It could be Laura Lyons. She lives in Coombe Tracey. She married an artist, but he left her. She works as a secretary now, but she doesn't make much money."

Dr Mortimer came with me to Baskerville Hall, and he stayed for dinner. Then Sir Henry and the doctor played cards, and I went to sit in the library. Barrymore brought me some coffee.

"Has your wife's brother found a ship?" I asked.

"I don't know," said Barrymore. "I hope that he has. I took food onto the moor three days ago, and it's gone now. But maybe the other man took it."

I stopped with the coffee cup in front of my mouth. "There's another man out on the moor? Have you seen him?"

"No. Selden saw him. The other man is hiding, too, in a **hut** on the moor. A boy brings him food from Coombe Tracey."

"Thank you, Barrymore," I said. I remembered the tall, thin man that Sir Henry and I saw in the night. Was it the same man?

The next morning, I went to Coombe Tracey. I found Laura Lyons' office, and went in. She was a beautiful woman with light hair. She was a secretary, so she thought that I had work for her.

"Hello," she said. "How may I help you?"

"I've come to ask you about Sir Charles Baskerville."

Her face went a little red. "What do you want to know?"

"Did you know him?"

"Yes. He helped me with money after my husband left," she said.

"Did you write to him?"

"Yes, I wrote to thank him," she answered.

"Did you meet him?"

Her face went redder. "Yes, once or twice, in

Coombe Tracey."

"Did you ask Sir Charles to meet you on the day of his death?" I asked.

Then her face turned white. I watched her mouth try to say "no".

"I know about the letter," I said softly. "You asked him to meet you at ten o'clock. Why did you want to meet at night – and in the garden?"

"He had to go to London for a few weeks," she said. "I wanted to see him before he left. He isn't married, so I didn't think that it was right to go inside his house with him."

"Why did you want to meet him?"

"Because I needed money quickly. I want to **divorce** my husband, and it can be very expensive."

"So you went to his garden. What happened?"

"I didn't go. That afternoon, another friend gave me money, so I didn't need to meet Sir Charles."

"But Sir Charles waited for you in the garden," I said. "And he died there!"

Laura Lyons looked down. "I know," she said. "And I feel terrible about it. I planned to write to him to explain, but then I read about his death in the newspaper the next day."

I thought that Laura Lyons' story might be true.

She asked to meet Sir Charles and then she didn't go because she didn't need to.

On the road back to Baskerville Hall, I saw a small boy in front of me, with a bag. He left the road and went out onto the moor. I remembered Barrymore's words about the other man on the moor. *"A boy brings him food from Coombe Tracey."* I followed the boy. He took the bag into a small hut, and then he went back to Coombe Tracey.

I had my gun ready, and I went into the hut. There was a bed, some food and water. There was also a table with a paper on it. I read these words:

Dr Watson has gone to Coombe Tracey.

I didn't move for a second. This man was watching me. I looked around the hut, but I didn't find any more papers. Was I in danger? Outside, the sun was low in the sky. I sat in a corner of the hut and waited, my gun in my hand.

Then I heard steps, and I saw a man come to the door. I heard a friendly voice say, "It's a beautiful evening, my dear Watson. Come outside. It's more comfortable than this hut. And please be **careful** with that gun."

CHAPTER SEVEN
Death on the moor

For a second I couldn't move.

"Holmes!" I said.

I stepped outside the hut, and there he was. He smiled, and his grey eyes danced as he looked at me. His face was brown from the sun, and he was thinner, but he looked very well.

"I'm very happy to see you," I said.

"And you're surprised?"

"Well, yes. Very surprised."

"How did you find me, Watson?" asked Holmes.

"I knew that there was someone on the moor," I said. "But I didn't know that it was you."

"You saw me one night, I think," said Holmes. "And today you followed the boy."

"Yes."

"And earlier you went to see Laura Lyons. You've helped me a lot."

"But why are you staying up here on the moor, in this old hut?" I asked.

"I wanted to watch things from outside," said Holmes. "And I didn't want our suspects to know that I was here."

"But why didn't you tell me? Don't you trust me?"

"Oh, Watson. I trust you a lot. I wanted to tell you, but then I thought – if I tell Watson, he'll want to help me. He's too kind. He'll visit me, and our suspects will see him. But I have all your letters – the boy brought them to me here. Together we're finding all the answers. What did you learn from Laura Lyons?"

I told Holmes about Laura's answers to my questions, and he was very interested.

"Did you know that she's very friendly with

Stapleton?" he asked me.

"No."

"They write a lot of letters, and they sometimes meet. If his wife knew—"

"His *wife*?"

"Yes. Beryl Stapleton is his wife, not his sister," Holmes told me.

"Why does Stapleton lie about this?" I asked.

"He wants people to think that they aren't married," said Holmes.

"So Stapleton is our suspect."

"Yes."

"And the letter to Sir Henry's hotel in London – did Beryl Stapleton make it and send it?"

"Yes."

"But how do you know this, Holmes?"

"You wrote to me about the Stapletons and their school in the north of England. It's easy to find information about schools. The teachers at that school were a husband and wife. They had a different name – Vandeleur – but the husband was interested in butterflies. Laura Lyons thinks that Stapleton isn't married, and you've discovered that she's divorcing her husband. That's because she wants to marry Stapleton."

"What will she do if she discovers that Stapleton is already married?" I asked.

"A good question, Watson, and it may help us. We'll go and see her tomorrow. But it's getting dark, and Sir Henry is alone at Baskerville Hall. You must get back there. Stapleton is planning a murder. We need to be ready before he—"

Suddenly, a terrible scream came from across the moor. Then we heard it again, only nearer.

"Where is it?" asked Holmes.

"There, I think." I pointed across the moor.

We heard the scream again, it was nearer now, and then the sound of a howl.

"We're too late, Watson," said Holmes. "Stapleton has done it!"

We ran across the moor and at the bottom of a hill, we saw a body. It was lying with its head turned in a horrible way.

"Look, Holmes," I said, as we got closer. "It's Sir Henry. Those are his clothes."

"He ran over that rock, fell and broke his neck," said Holmes. "But why did he come on the moor alone? Well, we can't help him, but we can still catch Stapleton." He looked at the body and turned the head. "What's this?" he said in surprise.

Then, he stood up, and suddenly he was laughing. "Look Watson. It isn't Sir Henry. It's Selden, the murderer."

"Barrymore gave some old clothes to Selden," I told him. "They were Sir Henry's. These boots, the shirt and the hat – they were all his."

"Selden died because of those clothes," said Holmes. "Remember Sir Henry's boot from the hotel? Stapleton took it, because he wanted the hound to learn Sir Henry's smell. And the clothes had that same smell, so the hound chased Selden."

"Why did Stapleton put the hound out onto

the moor?" I asked. "The hound isn't on the moor every night. So why did Stapleton think that Sir Henry was here tonight?"

"Yes, that's interesting," said Holmes. "But now we must do something for this poor man."

"Can you help me carry him to the hut?" I said. "Then I'll call the police."

"Yes. But wait a minute. Here comes Stapleton. Don't say that we suspect him – or our plans will be finished."

Stapleton was walking across the moor under the light of the moon. He saw us, stopped and then came on.

"Dr Watson," he said. "Why are you out here in the night? And what's this? Is somebody hurt? Oh, no, is it Sir Henry?"

He walked up to the body, looked down and then looked at me with surprise in his face.

"Who's this?" he asked.

"It's Selden, the prisoner."

We could see that Stapleton was not happy, but he tried not to show it. "How did he die?" he asked.

"He fell on some rocks and broke his neck," said Holmes. "We were walking on the moor and we heard a scream."

"Yes. I heard a scream, too," said Stapleton. "I came because I was worried about Sir Henry."

"Why did you think Sir Henry was on the moor?" I asked.

"I invited him to visit me, but he didn't arrive, and I was worried. And then I heard the screams. You heard the screams, too, you say? Did you hear another noise? The howl of a hound?"

"No. Why do you ask?" said Holmes.

"Oh, you know the old stories about a hound. I'm interested in them. So how did this poor man die? Did he fall?"

"He was alone on the moor for weeks," said Holmes. "He was tired, hungry and cold, and he had no hope. He went crazy, ran across the moor and fell."

"You're Sherlock Holmes, I think," said Stapleton. "Will you stay in Devon for long?"

Holmes smiled. "So you know me. No, I must go to London tomorrow."

"And before you leave, will you help us understand the strange death of Sir Charles, and now this poor man's death?"

"It's not an easy case," said Holmes.

Stapleton looked at Selden's body. Then he

turned to us. "Let's leave this man here, and I'll call the police in the morning."

"Thank you," said Holmes. "We must get back to Sir Henry."

We started on the path to Baskerville Hall, and Stapleton went back to his house alone.

CHAPTER EIGHT
The picture

Holmes and I walked across the moor in the dark. "We're getting very close to **solving** this," he said. "Did you see Stapleton's face? He was very surprised to see Selden, but he hid it very well. Stapelton's a clever man, Watson, and very dangerous."

"I'm sorry that he saw you."

"Yes, he may be more careful now. But he won't stop."

"Why don't we **arrest** him now?" I asked.

"We can't **prove** anything. Where's the hound? We don't know. And it's just a dog, it's not **proof** that Stapleton is trying to kill Sir Henry."

"But there's Sir Charles's death, too."

"He had a heart problem," said Holmes. "He died of fright, but we can't prove that the hound attacked or frightened him. And it's the same for Selden. We heard the hound, but we didn't see it. And we've no motive for the murder. Why did Stapleton kill Sir Charles and why does he want to kill Sir Henry?"

THE PICTURE

"So what do we do?"

"I have a plan for tomorrow, Watson. But now let's go to Baskerville Hall. We'll tell Sir Henry about tonight, but say nothing about the hound. I don't want to frighten him."

Sir Henry was very happy to see Holmes, but also surprised that he had no bags with him. Before supper, I went to visit the Barrymores.

"I'm sorry to tell you that Selden is dead," I told them. "He died on the moor this evening."

Mrs Barrymore began to cry. "You think that he was a bad man," she said. "And he *was* bad. But he was my little brother, and I always loved him."

I could say nothing to help her, and I left her with her husband. "He was a murderer," I thought, "but it's good that one person is crying for him."

I went back to the sitting room. Holmes was talking with Sir Henry.

"We thought for a minute that the dead man was you, because he was wearing your old clothes," Holmes told him.

"You've been busy, but I've had a boring day," Sir Henry told us. "Stapleton invited me to visit, but I couldn't go because you don't want me on the moor alone. So he's invited me and Dr Watson tomorrow evening. But how is the case? Have you solved it?"

"If you follow my plan tomorrow, I'll solve it," replied Holmes.

"Of course."

"If you . . ."

But suddenly, Holmes stopped talking and turned away from us. He was looking at the pictures on the wall – pictures of the Baskerville family. "Sir Henry," he said. "Can you tell me about these? Which one is Sir Hugo?"

THE PICTURE

Sir Henry pointed at one of the pictures. "This one," he said. "He was the first Baskerville to meet the hound."

Holmes looked hard at that picture, but he said nothing more. But after dinner, Sir Henry went to bed, and Holmes took me to look at Sir Hugo again. "Do you see anything?" he asked me.

"He looks a little like Sir Henry."

"Yes. But look at this." Holmes put one hand over the man's beard, and the other over his hair.

It was Stapleton's face!

"You see, Watson. Stapleton is a Baskerville. He's inherited the face of the terrible Sir Hugo. And he's as dangerous as Sir Hugo, too."

"And he plans to inherit the Hall," I said. "That's his motive!"

"Yes, Watson." Holmes was smiling now. "We'll catch Stapleton tomorrow. But now it's time for bed."

The next morning, Holmes and I had breakfast with Sir Henry, and then we talked about our plans for the day.

"Will you go to the Stapletons for dinner tonight, Sir Henry?" asked Holmes.

"Yes. And I hope you'll come," he replied.

"Watson's invited, and I'm sure that they'll be happy to see you, too."

"I'm sorry, but we can't. Watson and I must go to London. Sir Henry, please send a message to Stapleton. Say *Watson and Holmes can't come tonight. You must go alone.*"

"All right. But I'm sorry to see you leave," said Sir Henry, looking worried. "I thought that you planned to stay with me while I have this trouble."

"And after dinner at the Stapletons, I want you to walk home across the moor."

"But Mr Holmes," Sir Henry said coldly. "You asked me not to go on the moor alone."

"I know, but you must trust me," said Holmes. "It's not dangerous if you stay on the path. Watson and I are going to Coombe Tracey after breakfast, and then we'll take the train to London. But Watson will come back tomorrow."

THE PICTURE

At Coombe Tracey, we went straight to Laura Lyons' office.

"Mrs Lyons," said Holmes. "I'm working on the case of Sir Charles's death. You asked Sir Charles to meet you at the gate at ten o'clock and he died. This was murder. And we suspect that your friend Mr Stapleton and his wife are the murderers."

Laura Lyons jumped up from her chair. "His *wife*? But Mr Stapleton isn't married."

"He *is* married. Beryl Stapleton isn't his sister. She's his wife."

"It's not possible," cried Laura Lyons, angrily. "Prove it to me! Prove it to me!"

Holmes took something out of his pocket. "Here's a photograph. It's four years old, and it shows 'Mr and Mrs Vandeleur' in York, but you can see that they're the Stapletons. I'm sorry, Mrs Lyons, but they're married."

Laura Lyons looked at the photograph. "Mr Holmes," she said. "Stapleton asked me to marry him, but I needed to divorce my husband first. Stapleton lied to me, many times, for weeks and weeks. You suspect that he's a murderer. Can

I help you to prove it?"

"The letter that you wrote to Sir Charles," said Holmes. "Did Stapleton ask you to write it?"

"Yes. He stood behind me and watched me while I wrote it. I did it because I needed money for the **divorce**. But now I've hurt poor Sir Charles – and he was my kindest friend."

"And did Stapleton give you money that night and ask you to stay home?"

"Yes. He decided that he didn't want Sir Charles to help."

"But then Sir Charles died. Did you suspect anything?"

Laura Lyons looked down. "Yes, I did. But

I loved Stapleton – and I was frightened of him. So I said nothing to the police."

"You're a very lucky woman," said Holmes. "Stapleton is a dangerous man, and you were in great danger from him. But you're safe now."

We left Laura Lyons and walked to the station. "We're not going to London, Watson," said Holmes. "We're going to meet Lestrade, a detective from the London police. He's a very fine policeman, and I've asked him to help us."

The London train came into the station. A small man jumped out of a carriage and came to meet us. "It's good to see you again, Mr Holmes," he said. "Do you have anything good?"

"It's the biggest thing for years, Lestrade, and I'm happy that you're here," said Holmes. "Have you ever been to Dartmoor?"

"No."

Holmes looked up at the station clock. "You won't forget this visit, but first let's have dinner at Baskerville Hall. We still have two hours before we start."

CHAPTER NINE
On the moor

We took the carriage to Baskerville Hall. Sir Henry wasn't there – he was at the Stapletons'. Holmes showed his map to Lestrade at dinner and explained the case. Then we walked onto the moor in the dark.

"Do you have your gun, Lestrade?" asked Holmes.

"Yes," the policeman replied. "I'm always ready."

"Good," said Holmes.

We were getting near to the Great Grimpen Bog, and there was a thick **fog** over it.

"There are the lights of a house ahead," said Lestrade.

"Yes, that's the Stapletons' house," said Holmes.

We stopped about two hundred metres from the house and hid behind some rocks.

"We can see well from here," said Holmes. "Watson, you know the house. Can you go to a window and look inside?"

As quietly as possible, I moved nearer to the

house and looked in through a window. I watched for ten minutes and then went back to Holmes.

"What did you see?" he asked.

"Stapleton and Sir Henry are in the dining room, but I didn't see Beryl. Stapleton left the room for a minute and went outside. He went to a small hut in the garden and opened the door. Then I heard a strange noise, like an animal moving around. The door closed. Stapleton came back to the dining room and sat down."

"And Beryl Stapleton isn't there," said Holmes. "Where is she?"

"I don't know."

The fog over the Great Grimpen Bog was moving nearer to us.

"That fog is a problem," said Holmes. "I hope that Sir Henry leaves before it comes here."

But the fog was moving towards us quickly.

"He's coming," said Holmes, and we heard steps on the path. Sir Henry came out of the fog and went past, but he didn't see us behind the rocks. He walked quickly, and he looked worried.

"Listen," said Holmes, his gun in his hand. "Here's the hound."

I heard very quick steps. Something was

running on the path. We looked into the fog, Lestrade **screamed**, and then I saw something. It was an enormous black hound. Fire was coming from its face and open mouth, and its head and body were bright with a blue light. I've never seen anything so terrible in my life.

The hound ran down the path after Sir Henry, and Holmes and I both **shot** at it. The animal **howled**, but it did not stop. Down the path, I saw Sir Henry turn, his face white.

We ran after the hound, and I heard a scream from Sir Henry. At the same time there was a howl from the hound. Then it jumped on Sir Henry, its teeth above his neck. But Holmes shot again, five times, and the hound fell back. It was dead.

Sir Henry lay on the ground, but there was no blood on him, and he wasn't hurt. "What was that terrible thing?" he asked, his eyes white with fright.

"It's dead," said Holmes. "The Hound of the Baskervilles is dead."

The hound had a frightening blue fire on its mouth, head and body. I put my hand on the animal's head and saw cold fire on my fingers.

"**Phosphorus**," I said. "Stapleton made the fire and strange blue light with it."

"Very clever," said Holmes. "I'm sorry, Sir Henry,

because I put you in danger. But now we must find Stapleton. Wait here, and we'll come back soon and help you."

Sir Henry sat on a rock with his face in his hands while Holmes, Lestrade and I ran to the house.

The front door was open, and we went inside. We looked in all the rooms downstairs and then went upstairs. Lestrade suddenly stopped by one of the doors. "I can hear someone in here," he said.

We kicked the door hard, and it opened. We were in a strange room, like a museum. There were glass bottles with butterflies inside.

"Here's Mrs Stapleton," cried Holmes. "He's tied her to a chair!"

We quickly untied her. "My husband tied me here because I didn't want to help him," she said. "But is he safe? Has he escaped?"

"He can't escape us," said Holmes.

"No. I didn't mean my husband. Is Sir Henry safe?"

"Yes. And the hound is dead."

"Oh, thank you. You can see what he did to me." She showed us the angry red places on her arms. "But this is nothing. He made me crazy with his lies. It was OK when I thought that I had his love. But that was a **lie**, too. I wanted to stop him from hurting Sir Henry, but he was too strong. I loved him, but I don't love him now."

"Where will he go now?" asked Holmes.

"There's only one place. He'll go into the Great Grimpen Bog. In the middle, there's an island, with an old hut on it. The hound lived there, and there's a path through the bog to the hut. I can show you the path tomorrow. You can't follow him in the fog at night. It's too dangerous."

We left Lestrade at the Stapletons' house and took Sir Henry back to Baskerville Hall.

The next morning, Holmes and I went to the Stapletons' house, and Beryl Stapleton showed us the path into the bog. She stopped at its beginning, and Holmes and I carefully walked into it. It was dangerous, and I remembered the terrible cries of the wild horse that day with Stapleton. After some minutes, we saw a boot near the path. Holmes stepped into the bog to get it. His leg went down a long way, and I had to pull hard to get him back on the path. But he held up the boot, and we saw these words inside it "Meyer, Toronto, Canada".

"It's Sir Henry's boot. Stapleton threw it here," said Holmes.

"So we know that Stapleton was here," I said.

Then we saw footprints, but we didn't find Stapleton in the hut.

"He's dead," said Holmes. "He fell into the bog in the fog, and he's disappeared. He was a dangerous man, and the world is a safer place without him. Let's go home now, Watson."

CHAPTER TEN
Home in London

At home in London, Holmes and I talked about the case.

"I've done some more work on it, Watson," Holmes told me. "Stapleton was the son of Sir Rodger Baskerville, and he was born in Central America. He married Beryl Garcia in Costa Rica. Then he stole a lot of money from the government there, and he and his wife escaped to England. They used the name Vandeleur and opened a school near York. Stapleton started reading about his English family and heard about Baskerville Hall. He discovered that only two Baskervilles, Charles and Henry, came between him and the Baskerville money. So he had a strong motive, and he moved to Devon."

Holmes stood up and moved to the window with his pipe. "Stapleton heard the story of the Hound," he said, "and he discovered that Sir Charles had a weak heart. So he bought a dangerous hound and hid it on the island in the Great Grimpen Bog. He wanted Sir Charles to think that Beryl was his sister, and he asked her to be friends with him, but she didn't want to do that. So he used Laura Lyons to bring Sir Charles to the gate. Stapleton came with his hound, it ran at Sir Charles, and he died of fright. Stapleton took the hound back to the island and waited.

"Sir Henry came back from Canada, and Stapleton and his wife went to London. Beryl sent that strange letter to Sir Henry because she knew that he was in danger.

"Stapleton put on a beard and followed Dr Mortimer. It was important to take something of Sir Henry's because he needed his smell for the hound. So he stole Sir Henry's boot. But the first boot was new, so he had to steal a second, older one. The Stapletons went home with the boot, and you and Sir Henry went to Baskerville Hall.

"Stapleton was now an important suspect, and I came to Devon secretly to watch him. I had a boy to bring me food, your letters and to help me. The boy watched you, and I watched Stapleton. I soon understood Stapleton's plan, but I had no proof. We had to wait until that terrible night on the moor. But, Watson, we've solved the case, and we've talked enough about that criminal. It's time for dinner."

During-reading questions

CHAPTER ONE

1 How does Holmes know that Dr Mortimer is a young man?
2 What animal lives on Dartmoor?
3 Where did Sir Charles Baskerville die? What two things did Dr Mortimer and Mr Barrymore see near his body?

CHAPTER TWO

1 Why did Sir Henry inherit Baskerville Hall?
2 Why does Holmes think that someone is following Sir Henry?
3 Who do Holmes and Watson see in Baker Street? What is he doing?

CHAPTER THREE

1 Why is London more dangerous for Sir Henry than Dartmoor?
2 Who got some money when Sir Charles died and how much did they each get?
3 Who will inherit Baskerville Hall if Sir Henry dies? Does he want it?
4 How many boots does Sir Henry lose? Which one comes back?

CHAPTER FOUR

1 What does Watson hear in the night? Who is it?
2 Why does Stapleton go onto the moor?
3 What is dangerous on the moor, and why?
4 What does Beryl Stapleton want?

CHAPTER FIVE

1 Why does Watson follow Sir Henry onto the moor?
2 Why is Barrymore holding a candle to the window?
3 Sir Henry and Watson see two people on the moor. Who are they?

CHAPTER SIX

1 What does Selden want to do?
2 Who wrote a letter to Sir Charles and how do they know this? What did this person want from Sir Charles?
3 Who does Watson follow onto the moor, and what does this person do?

CHAPTER SEVEN

1 Who is staying in a hut on the moor, and why is this person staying there?
2 Why does Stapleton lie about his wife?
3 Who dies on the moor, and how does this person die?

CHAPTER EIGHT

1 Why can't Holmes and Watson arrest Stapleton?
2 What does Holmes show Watson in the picture of Sir Hugo Baskerville?
3 What does Holmes want Sir Henry to do after dinner with the Stapletons? Why is this strange?
4 Who do Holmes and Watson meet at the station?

CHAPTER NINE

1 What follows Sir Henry on the path? What does it look like?
2 Who do they find upstairs in the Stapletons' house? Why is this person there?
3 Where is Stapleton at the end of the chapter? What happened to him?

CHAPTER TEN

1 What was Stapleton's motive for coming to Dartmoor?
2 Why did Stapleton steal a boot? Why did he steal another boot?

After-reading questions

1 Holmes and Watson decide not to tell the police about Selden. Are they right to do this?
2 Why does Watson suspect Barrymore? Why does he stop suspecting him?
3 Stapleton tells people that Beryl is his sister, not his wife. This helps him with two things. What are they?
4 Can you think of three things that Beryl does to stop her husband's plan?

Exercises

CHAPTER ONE

1 Write the correct word in your notebook.

> hound   blood   chase   fright   heart
> howl   moor

1 ...*hound*.... a large, dangerous dog
2 .... to run after a person or thing. You try to catch it.
3 .... wild open country
4 .... a feeling of suddenly being frightened
5 .... It is red and goes around your body. It comes out if you cut your body.
6 .... a part inside your body
7 .... a long, loud noise from an animal, usually a dog

CHAPTERS ONE AND TWO

2 Complete these sentences in your notebook with the correct form of the verb.

1 I visited Holmes this morning, and he ...*was sitting*.... (**sit**) at the breakfast table.
2 One night, Sir Charles and I .... (**stand**) outside the hall. We saw a large black animal in the hills.
3 I left Holmes for the afternoon and .... (**come**) back in the evening.
4 Some strange things .... (**happen**) in the last few hours.
5 I .... (**lost**) a brown boot.
6 They were new boots. I .... (**buy**) them yesterday.
7 I .... (**hear**) about the hound many years ago.

CHAPTERS THREE, FOUR AND FIVE

3 Complete these sentences in your notebook, using the adverbs from the box.

| carefully | angrily | quickly | nearly | sadly | suddenly |

1 "No one has followed us," said Dr Mortimer. "We've watched everyone ..._carefully_... ."
2 "They've stolen another boot!" he shouted ....
3 I .... forgot that last night the place was sad and dark.
4 Sir Henry stood .... with his head down.
5 .... we saw another light out in the night.
6 He moved .... and disappeared into the dark night.

CHAPTER FOUR

4 Put the sentences in the correct order in your notebook.

a .... Beryl Stapleton runs after Watson.
b .... Stapleton invites Watson to his house.
c ..._1_... Watson and Sir Henry have breakfast.
d .... Watson and Stapleton see a horse go down into the bog.
e .... Watson has tea with the Stapletons.
f .... Watson hears the strangest sound he's ever heard.
g .... Watson meets Stapleton.
h .... Watson sees that Mrs Barrymore has red eyes.

CHAPTERS FIVE AND SIX

5 **Who says these words. Who do they say them to? Write the correct names in your notebook.**

1 "You can see the moor very well from here." ......*Watson*...... to ...*Sir Henry*....
2 "I must walk alone." .... to ....
3 "I love my sister very much, and I don't want to lose her." .... to ....
4 "Do you know a woman with the letters L.L. in her name?" .... to ....
5 "I needed money quickly." .... to ....

CHAPTERS SIX AND SEVEN

6 **Match the two parts of these sentences in your notebook.**

Example: 1 – d

1 If he attacks someone,
2 It will kill my wife
3 If he's out of the country,
4 If I tell Watson,
5 What will she do

a he'll want to help me.
b if she discovers that Stapleton is already married?
c if he goes back to prison.
d the police will know that he's here.
e then it's better for everyone.

CHAPTER SEVEN

7 **Write questions for these answers in your notebook.**
1 " _And you're surprised_ ?" "Well, yes. Very surprised."
2 "Why .... up here on the moor?" "I wanted to watch things from outside."
3 "..?" "Oh, Watson. I trust you a lot."
4 "Why .... about this?" "He lies because he wants people to think that they aren't married."
5 "Who ....?" "It's Selden, the prisoner."
6 "How ....?" "He fell on some rocks and broke his neck."

CHAPTERS EIGHT AND NINE

8 **Make these sentences negative in your notebook.**
1 "He'll stop." " _He won't stop_ "
2 "He died of fright."
3 "I want to frighten him."
4 "He's inherited the face of the terrible Sir Hugo."
5 "They'll be happy to see you."
6 "Stapleton is a dangerous man, and you were in great danger."
7 "We were getting near to the Great Grimpen Bog."
8 "We can see well from here."
9 "I can hear someone in here."
10 "He's tied her to a chair."

CHAPTER TEN

9 **Are these sentences *true* or *false*? Write the correct answers in your notebook.**
1 Stapleton was born in England. ....*false*....
   Stapleton was born in Central America.
2 Stapleton married Beryl Garcia.
3 Stapleton stole money from the British government.
4 Stapleton hid the hound at Baskerville Hall.
5 Beryl sent a letter to Sir Henry.
6 Stapleton stole Sir Henry's dog.

Project work

1 Write a page in Holmes's diary for the day that he meets Watson on the moor.

2 Write a newspaper report about one of these:
   a The death of Sir Charles
   b The death of Selden
   c The death of Stapleton
   d The old story of the hound on the moor.

3 Write an interview with Holmes about the days he spent in the hut on the moor.

4 Dr Mortimer wrote to Sir Henry in Canada after his uncle's death. Write the letter.

An answer key for all questions and exercises can be found at **www.penguinreaders.co.uk**

Glossary

alone (adj. and adv.)
There is no one with you. You are *alone*. *Alone* is the adverb of *alone*.

arrest (v.)
The police stop a person because maybe they did a bad thing. The police *arrest* them and take them to a police station.

believe (v.)
to be sure that something is true

blood (n.)
Blood goes around your body and comes out if you cut your body. *Blood* is red.

butterfly (n.)
A *butterfly* has six legs and four beautiful wings of different colours.

carefully (adv.); **careful** (adj.)
If you do something *carefully*, you think a lot about how you are doing it because you do not want to make a mistake or a bad thing to happen. You are *careful* because you do not want a bad thing to happen.

case (n.)
When a *detective* works on a *case*, they try to find information about a crime (= when someone does a very bad thing, for example, stealing something or killing someone).

chase (v.)
to run after a person or thing. You try to catch it.

danger (n.); **dangerous** (adj.)
If you are *in danger*, someone or something might hurt or attack you.

detective (n.)
A *detective's* job is to find information about a crime. A *detective* works for the police, or sometimes he or she helps the police, like Sherlock Holmes.

disappear (v.)
A person is there and you can see them. Then you cannot see them. They have *disappeared*.

divorce (v. and n.)
Married people *divorce* when they decide not to be together any more. They get a *divorce*.

escape (v.); **escaped** (adj.)
To *escape* is to run away from a person or place. An *escaped prisoner* has run away from a *prison*.

fall in love (phr.)
past tense: **fell in love**
to start to love someone

fog (n.)
a thick cloud all around you

fright (n.)
a feeling of suddenly being frightened

gate (n.)
a door between two fields, or in a garden. A *gate* is sometimes part of a wall.

hear (v.)
Someone tells you about something or you discover information about something. You *hear* about it.

heart (n.)
Your *heart* is a part inside you and it sends *blood* through your body.

hide (v.)
past tense: **hid**
1) You *hide* in a place because you do not want people to find or see you.
2) You *hide* something because you do not want people to find or see it.

howl (n. and v.)
A *howl* is a long, loud noise from an animal, usually a dog. *Howl* is the verb of *howl*. An animal *howls* when it is not happy.

hut (n.)
a small building with one room. A *hut* is usually made of wood.

inherit (v.)
1) to get money or other things from someone when they have died
2) You look like your parents or grandparents. You have *inherited* their face, or nose or eyes.

invite (v.)
to ask a person to visit your home or come to a meal, party, etc.

lie (-ing form *lying*) (v. and n.)
You say something but it is not true. You are *lying* or telling a *lie*.

map (n.)
a drawing of a place. A *map* shows roads and rivers, for example.

motive (n.)
why you do something. It is often a very bad thing. For example, you steal some bread because you are hungry. This is your *motive*.

neighbour (n.)
A *neighbour* lives near or next to you.

newspaper (n.)
You read about the news in a *newspaper*.

path (n.)
When many people walk over the same ground, their feet make a long, thin *path*. You walk on a *path* across fields, through forests, etc.

phosphorus (n.)
Phosphorus is yellow. It makes light in the dark and starts to make fire when you put it in the air.

prison (n.); **prisoner** (n.)
A person does a bad thing and they go to *prison*. If a person is in *prison*, they cannot leave it. They are a *prisoner*.

prove (v.); **proof** (n.)
To *prove* something is to show that it is true. *Proof* is the noun of *prove*.

scream (v. and n.)
If you *scream*, you make a loud, high noise with your voice. A *scream* is the noise you make when you are frightened.

servant (n.)
A *servant*'s job is to cook, clean or do other work in someone's home.

shoot (v.)
past tense: **shot**
to use a gun because you want to hurt or kill a person or animal

sir (n.)
You use the word *Sir* before the name of a man from a very rich and important family, for example, Sir Hugo.

solve (v.)
To *solve* a problem is to find the correct answer to it. For example, if a *detective solves* a *case*, they discover who did a crime (= when someone does a very bad thing, for example, stealing something or killing someone).

suspect (n. and v.)
The police try to discover information about a *suspect* because maybe they did a crime (= when someone does a very bad thing, for example, stealing something or killing someone). If you *suspect* something, you believe that something (often a bad thing) is true or will happen. If you *suspect* someone, you believe that maybe they did a crime.

trust (v.)
to be sure that someone is good and their words are true

weak (adj.)
not strong. If a person has a *weak heart*, their *heart* does not work well.